VIKING VOYAGERS

For Ffion and Eva

BIG PICTURE PRESS

First published in the UK in 2020 by Big Picture Press,
an imprint of Bonnier Books UK,
The Plaza, 535 King's Road, London, SW10 0SZ
www.templarco.co.uk/big-picture-press
www.bonnierbooks.co.uk

Copyright © 2020 by Jack Tite

1 3 5 7 9 10 8 6 4 2
1119 002

All rights reserved

ISBN 978-1-78741-419-8

This book was typeset in Graham and Quicksand
Illustrations were created digitally using shapes, colour and texture

Written by Jack Tite
Consulted by Chris Tuckley, York Archaeological Trust
Designed by Jack Tite, Marty Cleary & Kieran Hood
Edited by Carly Blake

Printed in China

VIKING VOYAGERS

Written & illustrated by Jack Tite

BPP

CONTENTS

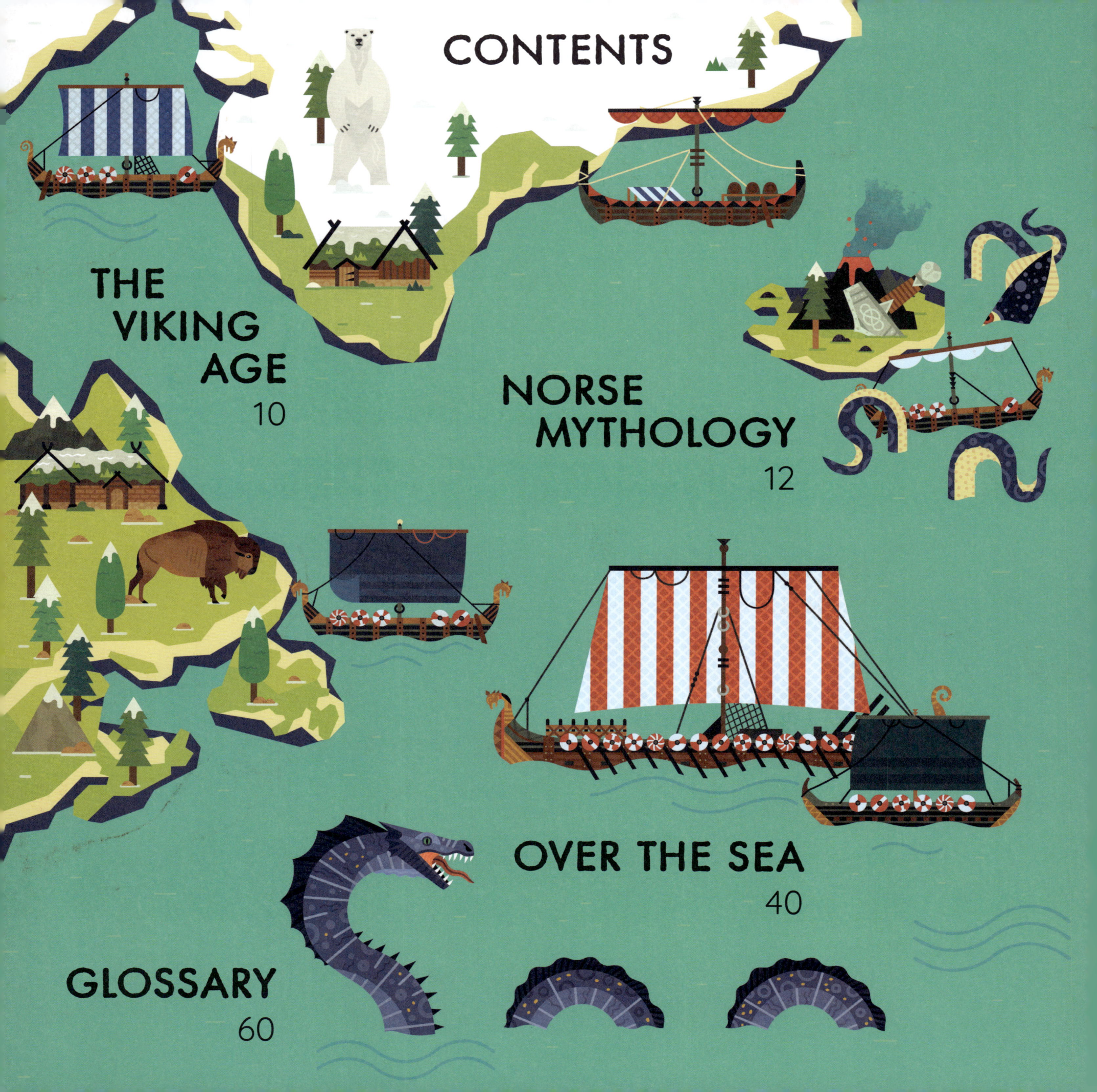

THE VIKING AGE
10

NORSE MYTHOLOGY
12

OVER THE SEA
40

GLOSSARY
60

HOME LIFE 22

LEGENDS 32

THE END OF AN AGE 52

N W E S

THE VIKING AGE

In the late 700s, hordes of people from Scandinavia left their homelands in northern Europe and ventured far and wide – the Viking Age had begun. In search of land and riches, they raided villages and towns across Europe with a previously unseen fighting force, which shocked the surrounding countries. Over the next 300 years, these legendary seafarers not only plundered, but also traded exotic goods, crossed oceans to explore new continents and settled in distant lands, including Britain, France, Iceland, Greenland and North America.

Northern Nations
The region in northern Europe that includes present-day Sweden, Denmark and Norway is known as Scandinavia, but these countries didn't yet exist at the beginning of the Viking Age. Instead, this region was made up of many different tribes and their settlements. These societies were very separate and tribes often fought each other for power, land and wealth.

Going Viking
Scandinavians did not call themselves 'Vikings'. This word stems from Old Norse, the language spoken in this region at the time. People who set off on ships to raid were called *víkingr*, and were said to be 'going viking' when they did. The name came to be used to refer to raiding Scandinavian seafarers from the late 700s to around 1100. In this book, 'Viking' refers to any Norse person during the Viking Age.

Viking travel routes (AD 1000)

- GREENLAND
- ICELAND
- NORTH AMERICA
- VINLAND (NEWFOUNDLAND)
- ATLANTIC OCEAN
- BRITISH ISLES
- SWEDEN
- NORWAY
- FINLAND
- Birka
- DENMARK
- Hedeby
- RUSSIA
- FRANKISH EMPIRE
- SPAIN
- BYZANTINE EMPIRE
- NORTH AFRICA
- MEDITERRANEAN SEA

■ Viking homelands
■ Places visited or settled
— Travel routes

A Bad Reputation

The Vikings' fearsome reputation as bloodthirsty warriors has stuck to this day, but the remarkable accomplishments they made should also not be forgotten. With the great need for boats – and lots of them – the Vikings revolutionised shipbuilding, and, in turn, became pioneers of exploration by setting foot in North America before any other Europeans. Get ready to meet these daring voyagers and discover what life was like.

NORSE MYTHOLOGY

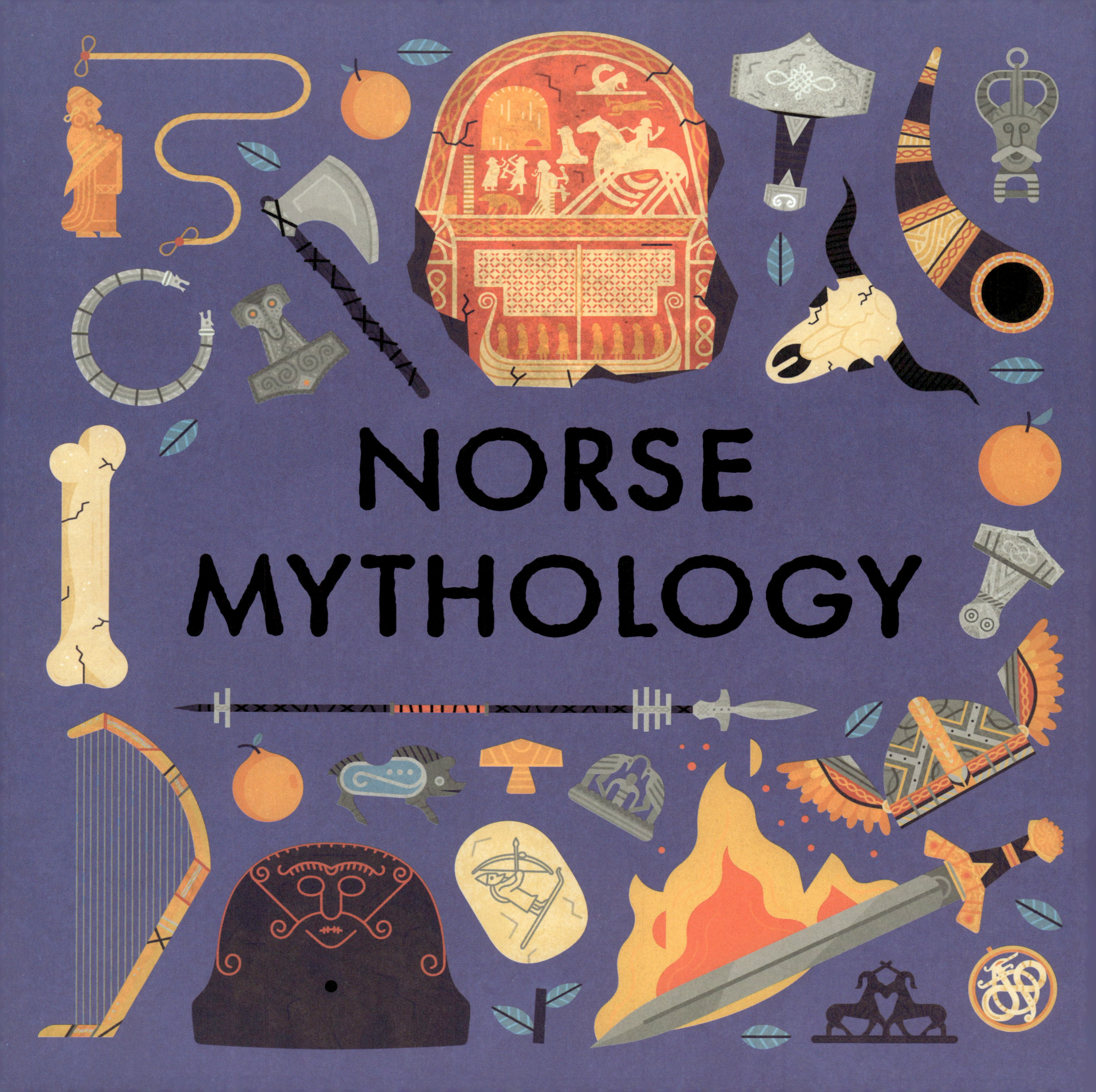

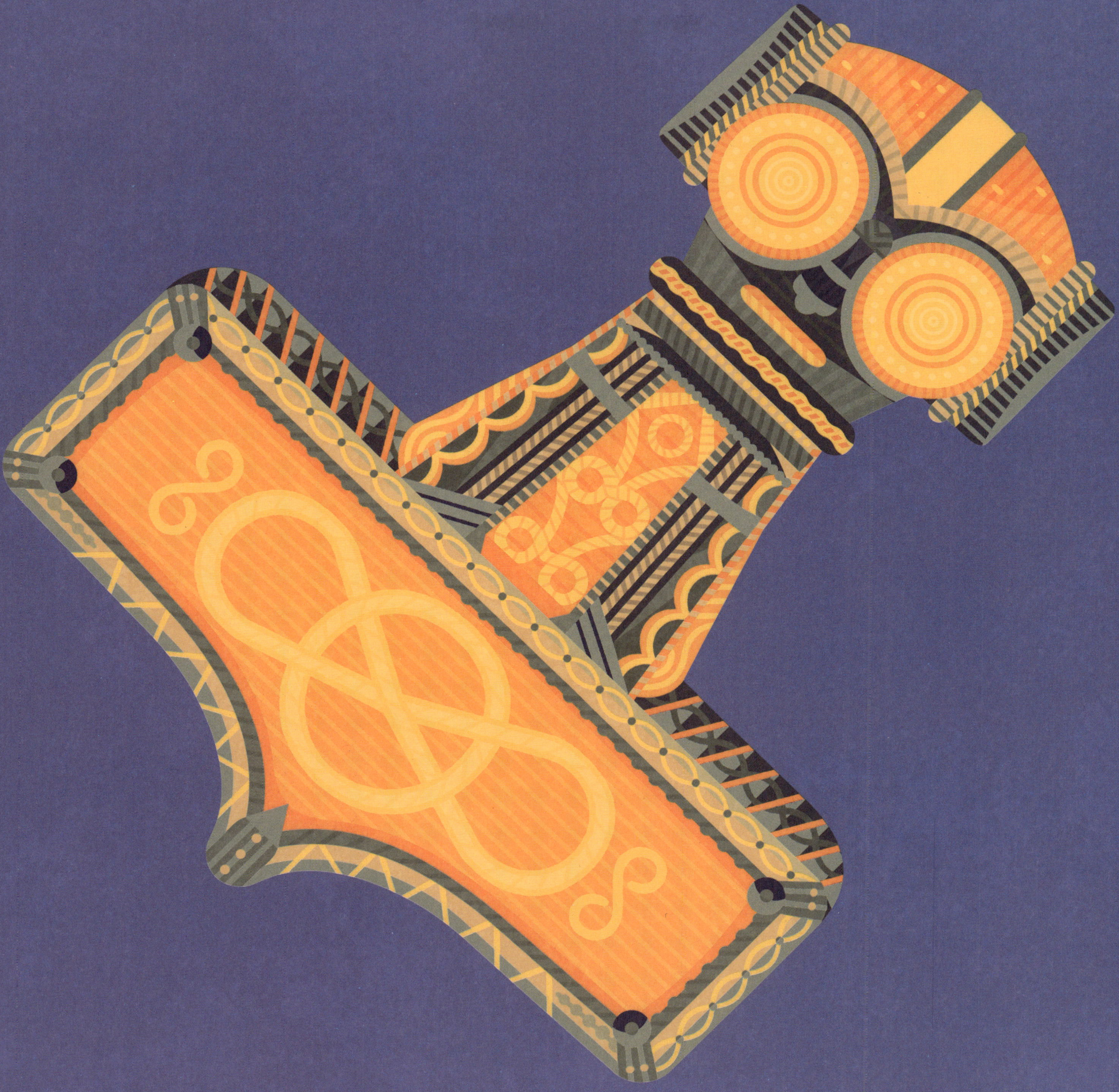

IN THE BEGINNING...

The Vikings had a rich faith centred around divine gods and goddesses and vibrant mythological stories. They believed that in the beginning, before there was anything, there was Ginnungagap – an abyss of emptiness so vast that no human could grasp its sheer size. To the north and south were two ancient realms – Niflheim and Muspelheim.

Opposites Attract

In the south, Muspelheim was a world so hot that no being could live there except for a fire giant named Surtr and his descendants. He guarded the blazing lands with his fiery sword. To the north of Ginnungagap was the freezing cold world of Niflheim, which means 'abode of the mist'. The two worlds slowly drifted towards each other, until the scorching flames of Muspelheim melted the ice of Niflheim.

When Worlds Collide

Droplets fell from Niflheim and formed the first frost giant, Ymir. Whilst Ymir slept, two more frost giants sprung from his armpits and one from his legs. The water droplets also created Audhumla, an enormous cow who produced rivers of milk. As Audhumla licked the blocks of ice, a man began to appear in them and three days later he was freed. His name was Buri and he was the first Norse god.

On the Shoulders of a Giant
Buri eventually had a son named Borr, who married the giantess, Bestla, and together they had three half-giant, half-god sons – Odin, Vili and Vé. The three siblings clashed with the frost giant, Ymir, and a great battle followed, ending with the giant's death. In Ginnungagap, the brothers created the entire world out of Ymir's body. They shaped the land from his flesh, the trees and grass from his hair, the mountains from his bones, the oceans and lakes from his blood and the rocks from his teeth, enclosing it all under a sky made from the giant's skull. From Ymir's eyelashes, the gods shaped Midgard – home of humankind.

Ash and Elm
Whilst walking along the seashore of their new world, the three gods came across two trees – an ash and an elm. Odin gifted the trees with life, Vili gave them feelings, Vé granted intelligence, and from them sprang the first humans. Odin and his brothers named the man Askr (Ash) and the woman Embla (Elm). These newly formed humans were the mother and father to all humankind.

DIVINE DEITIES

The Vikings believed in dozens of deities, most of which belonged to one of two main groups: the Æsir and the Vanir. Each god and goddess had a unique personality and power.

Mímir

A Wise Head
Mímir was the wisest of the gods. His magic well contained water that gifted wisdom to those who drank from it. In exchange for one sip, Odin sacrificed one of his eyes. Odin also sought advice from Mímir in times of need.

Odin

Ullr — Archery

Njord — Seafaring and wind

The All-Father
Odin, leader of the Æsir, was a wise god with one eye. He kept a check on Midgard with the help of two magical ravens. His wife and queen of Asgard, Frigg, was the goddess of wisdom and foresight.

Thor — Thunder and strength

Frigg

Heimdall — Guardian of Bifrost

Sif — Earth

The Son of Thunder
Thor, son of Odin and husband to the golden-haired goddess Sif, was hot-headed and strong. Two fierce goats hauled his chariot through the sky, creating thunder. His magical hammer, Mjölnir, was crafted by dwarves in Svartalfheim and one strike could flatten a mountain.

The Tree of Life
After Ymir's defeat, a great ash tree called Yggdrasil sprouted from his body. This tree is the centre of Norse mythology, with intertwining branches and roots that hold the nine worlds, each filled with different beings.

Asgard
High up in Yggdrasil is the glorious home of the Æsir – one of two main groups of gods which include Thor and Odin. Asgard is connected to Midgard by the Bifrost bridge.

Alfheim
A world of demigods, called elves, associated with nature and art.

Vanaheim
The Vanir – the group of magical land and sea gods – live in this world.

Bifrost bridge

Muspelheim
A blazing world inhabited by fire giants and demons. The fire giant Surtr, arch-enemy of the Æsir, guards this place with his fiery sword.

Midgard
The human world, which is surrounded by the great sea serpent Jörmungandr.

Niflheim
An ancient, frozen world of ice and mist.

Jötunheim
The rocky, mountainous dwelling of the giants.

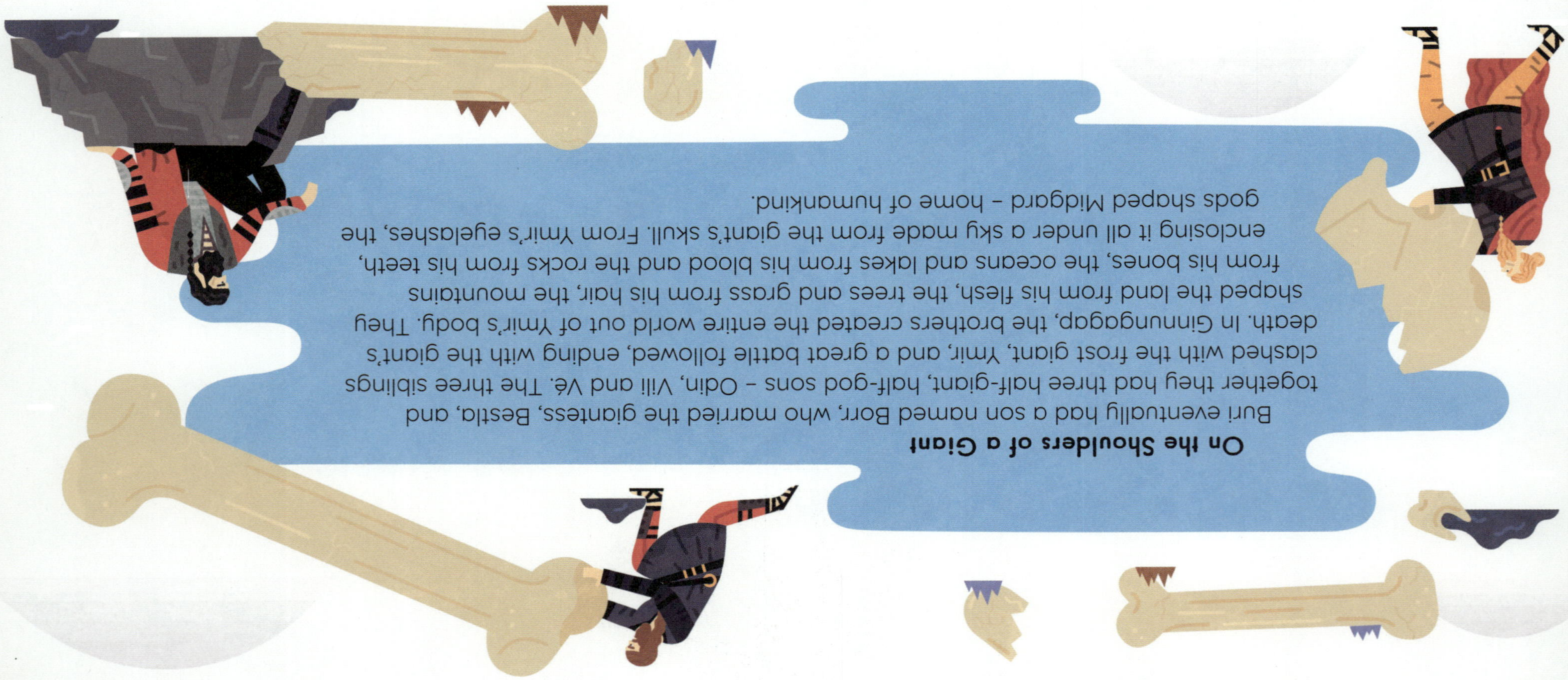

On the Shoulders of a Giant

Buri eventually had a son named Borr, who married the giantess, Bestla, and together they had three half-giant, half-god sons – Odin, Vili and Vé. The three siblings clashed with the frost giant, Ymir, and a great battle followed, ending with the giant's death. In Ginnungagap, the brothers created the entire world out of Ymir's body. They shaped the land from his flesh, the trees and grass from his hair, the mountains from his bones, the oceans and lakes from his blood and the rocks from his teeth, enclosing it all under a sky made from the giant's skull. From Ymir's eyelashes, the gods shaped Midgard – home of humankind.

DIVINE DEITIES

The Vikings believed in dozens of deities, most of which belonged to one of two main groups: the Æsir and the Vanir. Each god and goddess had a unique personality and power.

A Wise Head
Mímir was the wisest of the gods. His magic well contained water that gifted wisdom to those who drank from it. In exchange for one sip, Odin sacrificed one of his eyes. Odin also sought advice from Mímir in times of need.

Mímir

Odin

Ullr — Archery

Njord — Seafaring and wind

Thor — Thunder and strength

The All-Father
Odin, leader of the Æsir, was a wise god with one eye. He kept a check on Midgard with the help of two magical ravens. His wife and queen of Asgard, Frigg, was the goddess of wisdom and foresight.

Frigg

Heimdall — Guardian of Bifrost

The Son of Thunder
Thor, son of Odin and husband to the golden-haired goddess Sif, was hot-headed and strong. Two fierce goats hauled his chariot through the sky, creating thunder. His magical hammer, Mjölnir, was crafted by dwarves in Svartalfheim and one strike could flatten a mountain.

Sif — Earth

Bragi

The Poetic Prodigy
Gifted with beautiful poetry, music and wisdom, Bragi, husband of the goddess, Idun, was the poet and storyteller to the gods.

Rán

The ocean

War and love

Freyja

Tyr

Justice

Fertility and wealth

Freyr

Agriculture

Gefjon

Light and joy

Baldr

A Fable of Fruit
The goddess Idun had magical fruits, which the gods ate to stay young. In one tale, she was tricked by Loki and kidnapped by a giant, and without the fruits the gods grew old. The Æsir were angry at this, so they forced Loki to return Idun and then killed the wicked giant.

Idun

The trickster

Loki

Sacred Stories
The epic tales of the gods that tell of war, mischief, victory, love and sorcery in Norse mythology were an important part of Viking life. Vikings learned the myths by heart and passed them on to the next generation by reciting the stories out loud and carving runes (ancient letters) onto stones and other items. Most of the surviving written records that tell us about Norse mythology were made by foreign travellers who visited Viking settlements or Europeans who documented the period soon after the Viking Age ended.

17

THE CHILDREN OF LOKI

In Norse mythology, the mischievous shape-shifting trickster Loki was always getting the Æsir into trouble. He was the father of many fantastical offspring, including Odin's eight-legged horse Sleipnir, a monstrous wolf named Fenrir, Hel, the goddess of the underworld, and an ever-growing sea serpent called Jörmungandr. This water-dwelling beast is the biggest creature in the Norse world, even bigger than the giants of Jötunheim. Unsurprisingly, the gods were troubled by Loki's dangerous children. They banished Jörmungandr into the sea of Midgard, where its humongous body encircles the whole ocean with its head biting its own tail.

All Tied Up

The monstrous wolf, Fenrir, was said to have been raised from a small puppy in Asgard by the Æsir, so that the gods could watch over him. Fenrir grew at an alarming rate and his size struck fear into the hearts of the Æsir, so the gods declared that he should be tied and bound. When Fenrir broke free from two of the strongest chains with ease, the gods decided to use magical ropes crafted by the dwarves in Svartalfheim to try to keep him secured.

Beneath the Surface

The half-dead, half-living ruler Hel was exiled by Odin to Helheim, the underworld dwelling of the dead. Here, those who had lived a good-natured life and died from disease or old age were treated well, but those who committed bad deeds suffered in a snake-riddled, cold, gloomy place called Náströnd.

Out of Hand

The cunning gods pretended that they were tying Fenrir up to test his strength. Fenrir was not aware of the ropes' magic, but didn't trust the gods one bit. He allowed them to bind him *only* if one of the gods placed their hand in his open jaws as a gesture of good faith. Tyr, the god of law and justice, bravely put himself forward, but when Fenrir struggled to break free from the ropes, he bit off Tyr's hand. It was a worthy sacrifice – Fenrir was now bound securely and could cause no harm.

ASGARD

Asgard is one of the nine worlds and the home of many of the Norse gods. The Vikings believed this place to be a glorious paradise filled with heroic gods and goddesses. In Asgard, each god has their own land and a luxurious mansion made from gold or silver. A sturdy stone wall surrounds this realm, protecting it from the enemies of the Æsir – the giants.

Worlds at War

The Vikings believed that there were two groups of gods and goddesses: the Æsir, which included Odin and Thor, and the Vanir, which included Njord, Freyja and Freyr. At one point in time, they were at war. The Æsir were skilled warriors, whilst the Vanir fought with powerful magic. The two sides were evenly matched and after a long and costly war they called a truce and exchanged one god from each tribe to live in their new ally's world. From then on the two groups lived peacefully.

Hall of the Slain

One of the most iconic places in Asgard is Valhalla, a majestic hall with many rooms, a shield-covered roof, and rafters made of spears. Valhalla means 'Hall of the Slain', and this building is where Odin housed half of the most honourable Vikings who met their end in battle. The other half travelled to Fólkvangr, a field ruled by the goddess, Freyja. Every day the fallen warriors of Valhalla battle each other and each night their wounds heal and they feast.

Asgard Animals

Animals appear frequently throughout the Norse world, and Valhalla is no exception. Wolves guard the great hall's gates, whilst an eagle soars high above. A stag called Eikthyrnir and a goat called Heidrun are said to stand on the roof, eating the leaves from the highest branches of a golden tree called Lærad. Heidrun also supplies limitless amounts of an alcoholic drink called mead, which fallen Vikings chosen by Odin drink every night in Valhalla.

A Trickster's End
Asgard's vigilant guardian, Heimdall, will sound his horn to alert Asgard of the oncoming threat. On the battlefield, the unchained Loki will clash with Heimdall, and, after a fierce duel, they will slay each other.

Hammer Time
When Thor, god of thunder, and Jörmungandr clash, he will defeat the mighty serpent with an epic strike from his magical hammer. But, covered in the serpent's poison, Thor will then walk nine paces before he, too, falls.

Back to Ginnungagap
The prophecy also tells of the reversal of creation, when the burning worlds are destroyed and the vast void that is Ginnungagap is once more all that there is. Only a handful of gods, including Idun, Ullr and Sif, will survive Ragnarök.

A Brave New World
Although the Vikings believed Ragnarök was inevitable, life was prophesied to return. A new, lush world teeming with plants and animals will rise from the ashes after the war, ready for the surviving gods and two humans to start anew.

Ragnarök

Norse mythology tells of a prophecy known as Ragnarök – a series of future events ending in a great battle and the destruction of the world. It will begin when a furious Odin ties up Loki for tricking Odin's son, Hodur, into killing his own brother, Baldr.

Following three devastating winters on Midgard, the serpent Jörmungandr will emerge from the sea and shake the trunk of Yggdrasil to free Loki and his wolf-son, Fenrir. With armies of giants, they will journey to Asgard to face the gods and their valiant force of fallen warriors in a final battle.

Burning Bridges

The ferocious fire giant, Surtr, will wield his burning sword and strike the Vanir god, Freyr, killing him with a single blow. The fire giant will bring the fire of Muspelheim, which will engulf the nine worlds in flames and cause the oceans to boil.

Wild Wolf

Fenrir will fight with Odin and Tyr, but it will end with him devouring both gods. Vidar, another of Odin's sons, will avenge his father's death by grabbing Fenrir, pulling open his gaping jaws and plunging his sword into his mouth.

HOME LIFE

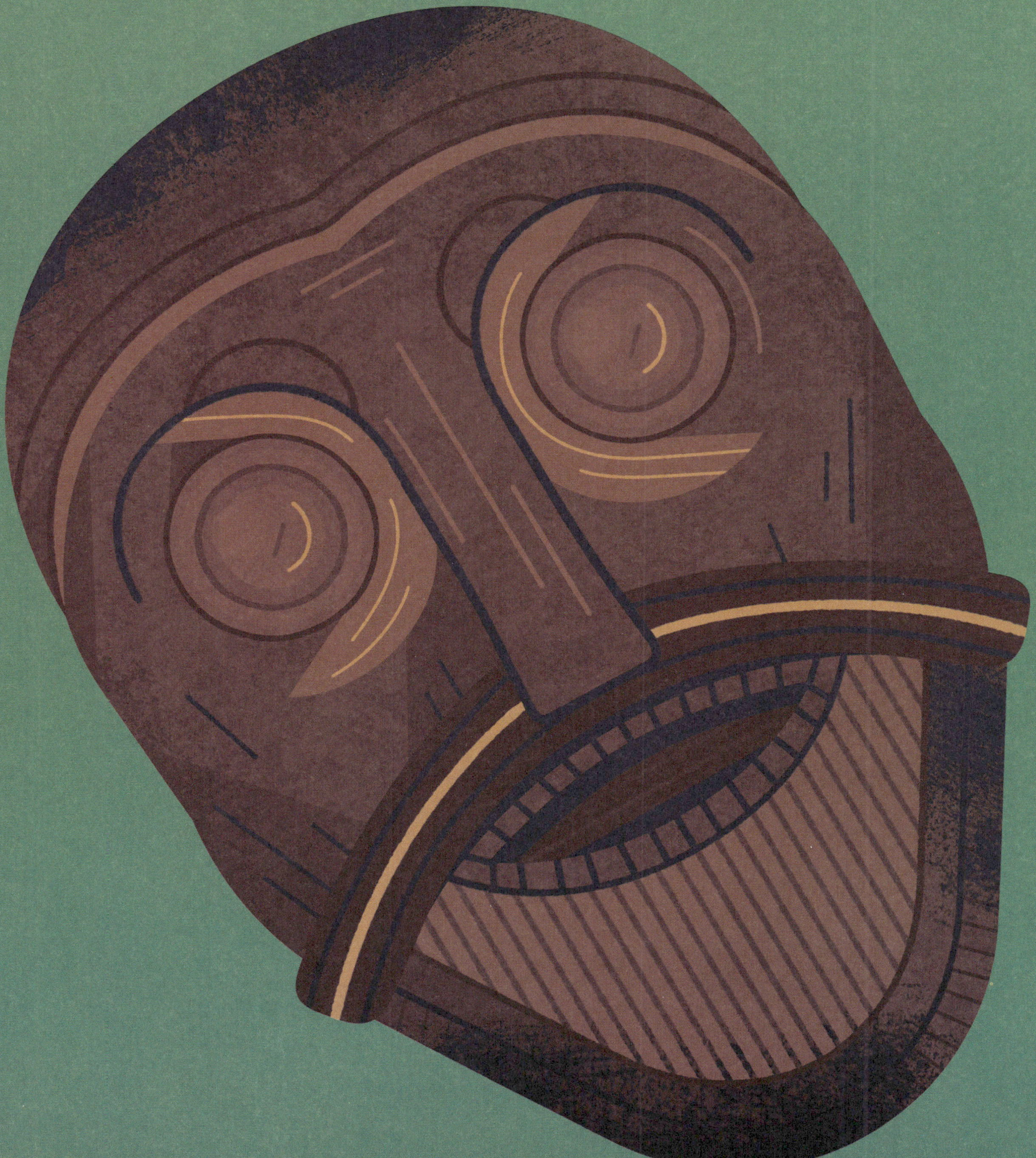

HOW VIKINGS LIVED

Most Scandinavians of the Viking Age lived simple lives on small farmsteads, growing crops and keeping animals. Each family lived together in a longhouse – a large rectangular building with a thatched roof. Men went out on expeditions, hunted for food and farmed the land, whilst women tended to oversee the household, craft clothing, cook meals and look after the family. After the Viking Age had begun, bustling trading towns gradually appeared across Scandinavia as raiding and trading with the rest of Europe continued.

Making a House a Home
Longhouses were crowded with children, parents and grandparents all under the same roof, and could be up to 70 metres long. Most homes contained just one large room, where the whole family ate and slept. The frame was made of timber, with stone, earth or wattle and daub (mud and sticks) for the walls. In Iceland, trees were scarce, so Vikings used stone for the walls and grass turf to cover the roof.

Living Off the Land
Fertile farmland provided the Vikings with a variety of home-grown crops. Harvesting could be a long and gruelling task, so the whole family, including children, often helped to gather in the food. As well as crop farming, Vikings kept animals, including cows, pigs and goats, for meat and milk; hunted wild deer, whales and even bears for meat and skins; and caught freshwater and ocean fish, too. They ate two meals a day, one in the morning and one in the evening. A typical Viking diet comprised of some of these foods:

- Hare
- Nuts
- Pork
- Bread
- Grains
- Beef
- Cabbage
- Seal
- Carrots
- Eggs
- Fish
- Pears
- Berries
- Crustaceans

LAW OF THE LAND

Society in the Viking Age had a social hierarchy with four distinct classes. At the top were the kings, who were high-achieving men that had shown heroic bravery or won great battles. Beneath the kings were the wealthy upper class, known as jarls. They owned large areas of land and ruled over their communities. Karls – simple farmers, craftspeople and warriors – lived under their jarl. At the bottom, thralls were slaves with few rights, who worked on farms and served their masters.

Fierce Females
Whilst the men were away on voyages or raids, women would have taken on all aspects of running the home, including hunting for food and looking after the farm or family business. Although most Viking women were homemakers, some enjoyed more freedoms than in other societies at the time, such as being able to own land. Several Viking sagas, epic stories of adventure, speak of shield-maidens – fierce female warriors devoted to warfare, but it is still debated whether women fought in battle.

King

Jarls

Karls

Thralls

Living Off the Land

Fertile farmland provided the Vikings with a variety of home-grown crops. Harvesting could be a long and gruelling task, so the whole family, including children, often helped to gather in the food. As well as crop farming, Vikings kept animals, including cows, pigs and goats, for meat and milk; hunted wild deer, whales and even bears for meat and skins; and caught freshwater and ocean fish, too. They ate two meals a day, one in the morning and one in the evening. A typical Viking diet comprised of some of these foods:

Hare · Nuts · Pork · Bread · Grains · Beef · Cabbage · Seal · Carrots · Berries · Pears · Eggs · Fish · Crustaceans

A Warm Hearth

At the heart of a longhouse was the hearth – a stone fireplace where the family gathered to cook, eat, share stories and stay warm. In winter, temperatures plummeted, so animals were brought inside to shelter.

Under Lock and Key

Vikings kept their valuables locked away in chests. The women looked after the keys and were responsible for the family's treasure. They wore them on the outside of their clothing as a symbol of their key-bearer status and power.

On the Inside

With no windows, the walls were decorated with animal pelts, shields, clay lamps and woven hangings. Furniture was simple, wooden and ideal for limited space, with benches doubling as beds. Weapons and tools would have been hung up off the ground.

LAW OF THE LAND

Society in the Viking Age had a social hierarchy with four distinct classes. At the top were the kings, who were high-achieving men that had shown heroic bravery or won great battles. Beneath the kings were the wealthy upper class, known as jarls. They owned large areas of land and ruled over their communities. Karls – simple farmers, craftspeople and warriors – lived under their jarl. At the bottom, thralls were slaves with few rights, who worked on farms and served their masters.

King

Jarls

Karls

Thralls

Fierce Females

Whilst the men were away on voyages or raids, women would have taken on all aspects of running the home, including hunting for food and looking after the farm or family business. Although most Viking women were homemakers, some enjoyed more freedoms than in other societies at the time, such as being able to own land. Several Viking sagas, epic stories of adventure, speak of shield-maidens – fierce female warriors devoted to warfare, but it is still debated whether women fought in battle.

Dead and Buried

The Vikings believed that after death they went to an afterlife, so funeral preparations were highly important. The dead were given a full burial or they were cremated, with the belief that the smoke carried them to the next world. Your funeral depended on what status you held in society. Important Vikings who died in battle hoping to reach Valhalla after death were sometimes buried in boats. Valuable objects from life were placed in the person's grave – farmers have been found buried with tools, warriors with their weapons and women with jewellery, but thralls would have had few or no possessions to be buried with.

Karl farmer burial

Uppsala ship burial

Grave Goods

The high classes, such as jarls and kings, were usually laid in a boat after death, furnished with treasures and possessions to ensure a safe journey to the afterlife. In addition to valuables, beloved pets or animals were sometimes buried alongside their masters to serve them in the next world.

Bygone Burials

Many ship burials have been found all over Scandinavia and in England, Scotland and Eastern Europe. In July 2019 in Uppsala, Sweden, an intact boat burial was discovered containing the remains of a Viking man with a horse and a dog next to him and many weapons and trinkets. This burial was likely for a wealthy chief. Other known burial boats can be humongous, such as the lavish 1,200-year-old Oseberg ship found near Tønsberg in Norway, which measured 21 metres in length. On board were two female skeletons, a carved wooden cart, ornate sleighs, tools, textiles, precious treasures, fifteen horses, six dogs and two cows.

VIKING ANIMALS

Vikings kept animals for many uses, not only for food. Dogs were used by farmers to herd animals, whilst the wealthy kept exotic creatures such as peacocks to show their status. Written records describe the importance of animals, and burials found with pets alongside their owners show us this too.

A Buzzing Business
In southern parts of Scandinavia, where the climate was warmer, people kept bees. The honey was brewed with water to make an alcoholic drink called mead, which was widely traded across Europe and made for a profitable business.

Killer Kittens
Native wild Scandinavian cats, known as skogkatt, were larger and fiercer than today's domestic cats. Vikings prized their excellent hunting skills and kept them in the home to keep living areas free from mice and rats. Cats were also taken on voyages to rid the ships of pests.

Canine Companions
The Vikings kept a variety of different dogs for hunting, herding and companionship. The strongest canines were trained to help hunt large prey, such as moose and bears, whilst others were trusty trackers that could follow a scent for long distances.

House Bears
It may have not been uncommon for brown bears to be kept as 'house bears'. Cubs would have been taken from the wild and raised in a family home, but as they got older and larger house bears would have become a nuisance. In Iceland and Greenland, polar bears were sometimes domesticated, but they were seen as an extravagant pet. Wealthy Vikings in these icy regions occasionally gifted them to European kings for favour and fortune in return.

Magical Makers

Viking finds, from homeware such as pottery and glass, to armour and weaponry, required specialist skills and tools to craft. The Jelling Cup is an ornate silver chalice dating back to the 950s and was discovered in a burial mound in Jelling, Denmark. It is thought to belong to the king, Gorm, and his wife, Thyra. Here are some of the many objects Vikings crafted:

Jelling Cup

Pottery

Fun and Games

Vikings made their own musical instruments to play, such as the pipe, flute and lyre (a wooden stringed instrument). Archaeologists discovered a tenth-century bone flute in Birka, Sweden, that is still playable today. Board games were also a popular activity and in Scotland in 1831 the 'Lewis chessmen' were unearthed – a set of chess pieces from Scandinavia carved from walrus ivory and whale teeth dating from the 1100s.

Travelling Tools

Wooden skis and animal-bone ice skates were efficient ways to travel in Scandinavia, and fun pastimes, too. In Reinheimen, Norway, a well-preserved ski that had been frozen in the ice for 1,300 years was discovered. It is thought that this was from a pair used by a skiing Viking.

Reinheimen Skis

Clothing

Lyre

Birka flute

Lewis chessmen

Dressed to Impress

Women spent their time spinning wool on a loom to weave clothing such as tunics, trousers and dresses. Cloaks, silk, animal furs and leather were also worn, with belts and brooches to fasten fabric together. Vibrant colours were fashionable and clothing was dyed with yellow, purple, red and blue pigments extracted from plants. Many clothes were waterproofed with fish oil as a final touch. Clothing finds are rare because they decay quickly, but some well-preserved examples have been found in graves.

CURIOUS CREATIONS

The range of artefacts that have survived from this period show us how rich Viking culture was. They were skilled craftspeople and created many intricate items, from pottery and jewellery to musical instruments and deadly weapons. The language of the Vikings is called Old Norse and the 16 letters, or runes, in its alphabet form what is known as the Futhark alphabet. The Vikings didn't write on paper, but instead made carvings into stone, wood, bone and decorative items.

Storied Stones

More than 3,000 runestones can be found in Europe, with most located in Scandinavia. These great stones bear elaborate carvings and were painted in bright colours, which have since faded. Some mark important events or people, whilst others tell stories with the images and runes they depict. They were stood in busy places, often near roads and bridges.

A Jelling Stone with reconstructed colour

Crafted items

Written in the Runes

A huge runestone was raised in the village of Jelling in Denmark, around 965 by the King Harald Bluetooth. He succeeded in unifying Denmark under one ruler and bringing about Christianity, and this stone is inscribed with an account of these events. It stands next to one other stone, and together they are known as the Jelling Stones.

Raven Relay
These iconic black birds feature in carvings, on Viking flags and shields and in Norse mythology. The chief god Odin owned two ravens that flew around Midgard, relaying news back to the god.

Bountiful Birds
Wealthy Vikings in Greenland, Norway, Sweden and Iceland bred and trained falcons to hunt small prey as a sport and exported them across Europe. Owning a gyrfalcon, the largest falcon, was seen as the ultimate statement of power by European kings.

Exotic Exports
Peacocks brought to Europe from as far afield as India were kept by the rich to show off their wealth and trading links. Two were found in the grand ship burial of a man in Gokstad, Norway, alongside two hawks, eight dogs and twelve horses.

Wild and Woolly
Sheep provided milk, meat and wool. Iron shears were used to cut a sheep's wool, or it was plucked. The Manx Loaghtan, a rare breed that had up to six horns, was one of the best for wool because it shed naturally. This sheep was introduced to Britain by Viking farmers, and today is only found on the Isle of Man.

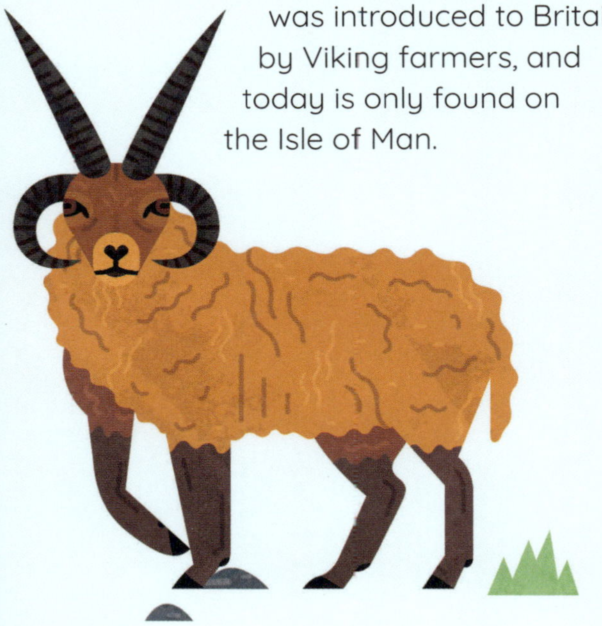

The Sacred Cow
Cattle were farmed for their milk, meat and hide, and were also used to pull carts to transport goods. Among other animals, bulls were sacrificed as offerings to the gods at ceremonies.

Farm Life
Horses, pigs, poultry and goats could also be found on a typical Viking farm and, in Northern Europe, herds of reindeer, too. The number of animals a Viking kept was seen as a measure of wealth – the richest people owned hundreds of farm animals.

29

Taking up Arms

Most warriors would have carried a spear and a shield, but wealthy Vikings could afford swords. Those that had the name 'Ulfberht' on their blade were some one of most sought after types, because this maker's name was a mark of superior strength and sharpness. In battle, warriors wore leather armour, sturdy chain-mail tunics and domed iron helmets. (There is no archaeological evidence of Vikings wearing horned helmets).

Precious Relics

Jewellery was made from precious metals, such as bronze and gold, and decorated with shells, amber and rare minerals such as jet. Amulets featuring Thor's hammer and other mythological symbols were worn to show their beliefs, while jewellery such as ornate rings showed off wealth. The Vikings also carved elaborate carts, sleighs and other wooden objects. The Oseberg cart dating from 800 or earlier is carved with images of cats, serpents and fierce-looking faces.

Being Clean

Hygiene was a high priority for Vikings. Combs made of antler or bone and metal tweezers have been common finds. A comb case was found engraved with runes that read: 'Thorfast made a good comb'. It was probably written by the craftsman himself over a thousand years ago! The Old Norse word for 'Saturday' means 'bathing day', and weekly bathing was the norm, which was more than many other societies of the day.

Spear · Bow · 'Ulfberht' sword · Shield · Armour · Axe · Drinking horn · Thor's hammer · Oseberg cart carving · Thorfast's comb · Jewellery

Fascinating Finds

Archaeologists have unearthed tens of thousands of Viking objects across Europe, including cups, swords, chests, coins and combs. Along with smaller objects, mass graves, whole carts and remnants of longhouses have also been discovered.

A King's Hoard

In January 2018, a 13-year-old boy and his teacher were scouring a field with a metal detector on the German island of Rügen, when they came across a shiny piece of metal. Scientists identified it as a silver coin originating from a Viking trading town called Hedeby in Denmark. It was soon discovered that this single coin was part of a much bigger find...

LEGENDS

Fascinating Finds

Archaeologists have unearthed tens of thousands of Viking objects across Europe, including cups, swords, chests, coins and combs. Along with smaller objects, mass graves, whole carts and remnants of longhouses have also been discovered.

The Rügen hoard contained hundreds of objects, including jewellery, pearls, brooches and coins. Of the 600 coins, the oldest is a Damascus dirham from the Middle East, which dates back to 714. Some historians believe that this treasure trove was buried by ruler of Denmark King Harald Bluetooth in the 980s whilst he was fleeing from a crippling defeat by his own son, Sweyn Forkbeard.

LEGENDS

A King's Hoard
In January 2018, a 13-year-old boy and his teacher were scouring a field with a metal detector on the German island of Rügen, when they came across a shiny piece of metal. Scientists identified it as a silver coin originating from a Viking trading town called Hedeby in Denmark. It was soon discovered that this single coin was part of a much bigger find....

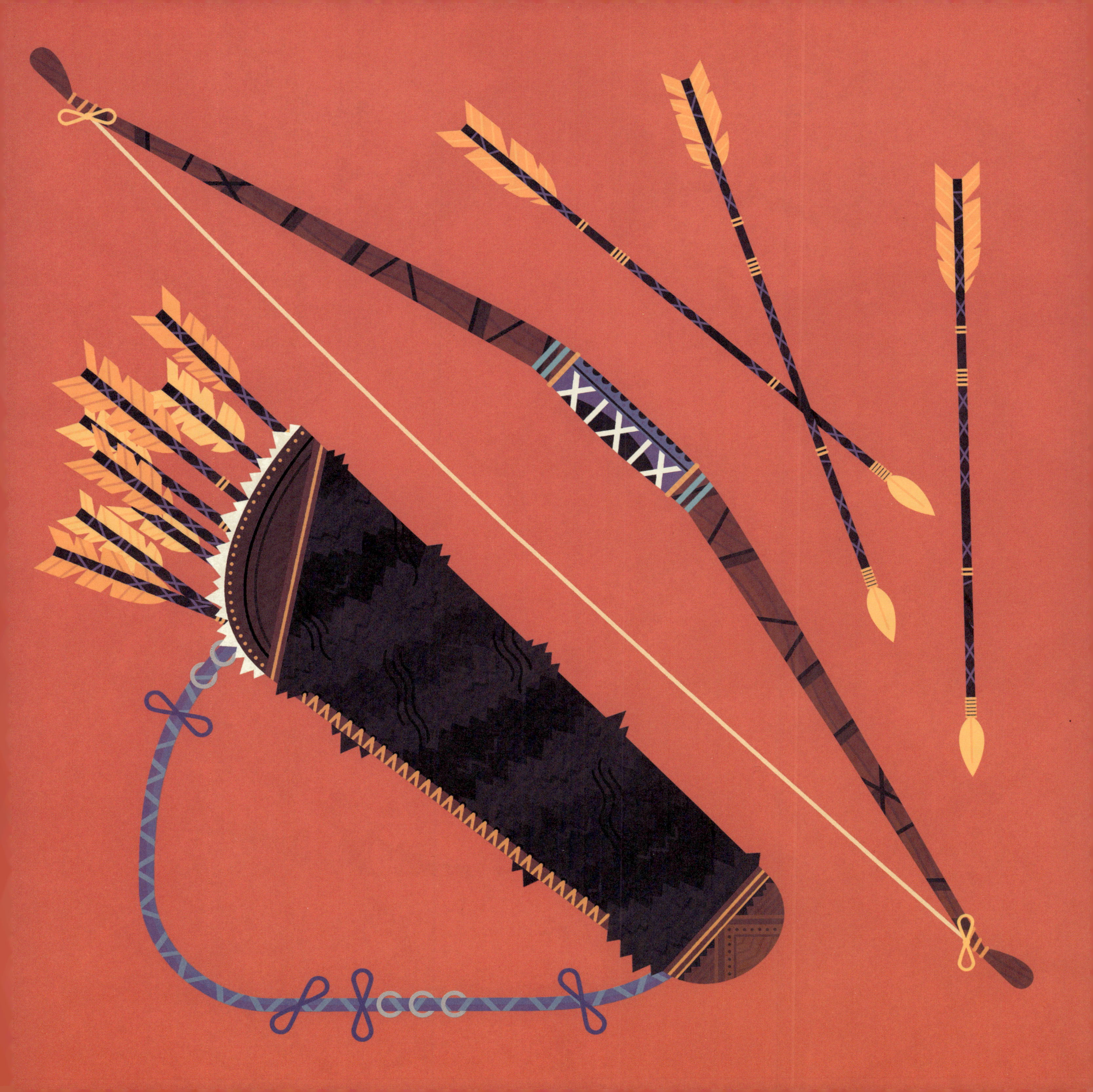

GRETTIR THE STRONG

Few tales feature more monsters than that of the Icelandic outlaw named Grettir, an epic saga that spans 93 chapters. Grettir, who was clever and courageous but quick-tempered, grew up beloved by his mother but disdained by his wealthy father, Asmund Longhair. At the age of 14, he was exiled from his home over a dispute, and Grettir decided to go on a journey. Before Grettir set sail, his mother gifted him with a powerful, ancient sword that had belonged to her grandfather, Jokull, and with that his adventure began.

Karr the Old
His first stop was an island ruled by a great chief named Thorfinn, son of Karr the Old. Grettir had heard of the treasure-laden grave of Thorfinn's father and was determined to take its riches, but Karr haunted the island as a draugr – an undead creature with great strength. While digging up the grave, Grettir was seized by the draugr. The pair struggled and fought, but eventually Grettir sliced Karr's head off with his sword.

A Bad Bear
In Norway, Grettir scaled a high cliff to hunt down a deadly bear that had been terrorising the nearby farm. The bear spotted Grettir as he approached the den and the fierce animal charged out. With a well-timed swing of his sword, Grettir cut off the beast's paw and they both tumbled over the cliff's edge, crashing down onto rocks. By a stroke of luck, Grettir landed on the bear and survived the fall.

The Tale of Two Trolls
One winter, Grettir arrived to stay at a farm haunted by trolls. Late one night, a giant she-troll attacked Grettir and they clashed, destroying half of the farm in their brawl. The hero sliced off the beast's arm and she fell into a nearby waterfall. Grettir searched in the waterfall and deep below he found a huge cave – and in it another troll! He swiftly slashed at his enemy until the troll was defeated. Thanks to Grettir, trolls no longer tormented the farm after that.

Back from the Dead

Grettir came upon yet another farm plagued by deaths. The owner told him of Glam, a towering man who he had hired as a shepherd. Glam had been mysteriously killed and had returned from the dead as a ruthless draugr to haunt the land, killing animals and sometimes the workers. One night, Grettir patiently waited in one of the houses for Glam to come for him...

Glam's Curse

Over the whistling wind, the sound of footsteps approached Grettir and the menacing figure of Glam loomed over him. The monstrous draugr grabbed Grettir with all his might, wrestling him about the house and dragging him outside. The hero regained his footing and grasped his sword, outwitting Glam. The draugr was defeated, but he cursed Grettir never to have peace and to live the life of an outlaw. Grettir answered with a final blow and Glam's head fell to the floor, but he now had a troubling curse to worry about.

The Outlaw's End

Grettir became an outlaw for 20 long years, fighting off attacks from bounty hunters and warriors to survive. He only knew bad luck and loneliness, living his final days on the island of Drangey, Iceland. Displeased by Grettir, a witch cast a curse on him with runes carved into a tree stump and soon afterwards he badly injured his leg. The wound slowly worsened, Grettir's health got worse and the witch's foster-son returned and slayed Grettir. Soon after, Grettir's half-brother tracked down the killer, to avenge the hero who had helped so many during his life. He is known as Grettir the Strong.

SIGURD THE DRAGON SLAYER

According to legend, Loki, Odin and the god Hoenir were wandering Midgard when they stumbled upon an otter fishing at a waterfall. Loki killed the creature and took its pelt to a local dwarf named Hreidmar hoping to trade it for a night's stay in his home. However, the dwarf and his two sons, Fafnir and Regin, were outraged when they saw the offering – the creature was Hreidmar's third son, who had shape-shifted into the form of an otter. Odin made peace by promising the grieving father an impressive hoard of gold. Reluctantly Hreidmar accepted the gift from the gods.

The Cursed Ring

Loki travelled to Svartalfheim to meet a dwarf named Andvari, where he demanded riches from the underground caves to give to Hreidmar. Andvari would not hand over his hard-earned treasure and transformed into a fish to escape. Loki caught him, and Andvari finally agreed to give him his hoard – but saved one ring for himself. But Andvari didn't fool the cunning god and Loki demanded the dwarf give him this trinket, too. Andvari handed it over, but as he did he cursed the ring to destroy anybody who possesses it.

Fafnir's Transformation

The gods returned to Hreidmar and gifted him with the treasure, but the cursed ring had already began to work its magic. Fafnir was soon driven mad by greed and he killed his father, Hreidmar, to claim the riches for himself. After this evil deed, Fafnir transformed himself into a monstrous dragon and took the hoard to a lair that he kept guard over.

The Search for a Steed

Hreidmar's son, Regin, became a blacksmith and fostered a young boy named Sigurd, who he raised to be brave and strong. Sigurd was in the woods one day in search of a horse of his own, when he came across an old man with one eye. The man helped Sigurd, offering him a grey horse that he said was a son of Sleipnir, Odin's eight-legged steed. The man knew this because he himself was Odin in disguise. Sigurd took the horse and named it Grani.

Weapon of Choice

One day, Regin told Sigurd of Fafnir's fortune. Sigurd felt angry and decided he would defeat the dragon – he just needed the right sword. Regin used his smithing skills to forge two blades, which he tested by striking them on an anvil. Both shattered, so Regin crafted a third from Sigurd's broken sword. This ancient blade, named Gram, had belonged to Sigurd's real father. When Sigurd swung this sword with all his might, Gram split the anvil in two. He now had all he needed to defeat Fafnir.

Slaying the Serpent

Fafnir came out from his lair in search of water, unknowingly slithering over Sigurd's hiding place and rumbling the earth around him. Sigurd thrust his sword straight into the dragon's heart. Fafnir thrashed around and spat out fire and venom, but his last words were a warning to Sigurd: "Ride away from the treasure whilst you still can, or it will be your doom".

The Curse Continues

Regin had been hiding behind the bushes all along and came over to his slain brother, Fafnir. He asked Sigurd to roast Fafnir's heart and Sigurd did so. Sigurd tasted the dragon's heart while it was cooking and suddenly he found that he understood the chattering birds. They told him that Regin had intended to betray him from the beginning to keep the treasure for himself. When he learnt this, Sigurd drew Gram and killed Regin, before loading up as much treasure as Grani could carry – including the cursed ring.

Dig In

Once Sigurd was ready, he prepared for the battle ahead by digging a hole close to Fafnir's lair where he could hide. Whilst digging, Odin visited Sigurd, in disguise as an old man again, and advised him to dig many pits in order to contain the dragon's blood once he had killed his enemy. Sigurd took Odin's advice and dug ditches around Fafnir's dwelling, then patiently waited for the monster to emerge.

ARROW-ODD

Arrow-Odd's saga is an epic Icelandic tale from the 1200s, which features the first ever mention of the kraken. Odd, son of Grim Hairycheeks, grew up in Norway. As a boy, a witch predicted that he would die in his hometown caused by his horse, Faxi. This terrified Odd, so he struck the witch in the face with a stick, killed his beloved Faxi and set out on a sea-roving quest seeking wealth and adventure with his brother, Thord. Before he set sail, Odd's father gifted him with a sheath of magical arrows that flew of their own accord, always hit their target and returned to their bow.

Making Waves
Odd sailed all over Northern Europe with his crew, raiding lands, battling monstrous beasts and overthrowing kings. They even ventured into Jötunheim, land of the giants, to fight any enemy brave enough to face them.

Dressed to Kill
In Ireland, Odd met his wife, Olvor. She crafted him a magical shirt embroidered with gold that stopped him feeling cold, hungry or tired. It also protected him from fire and iron weapons in battle – unless he was running away.

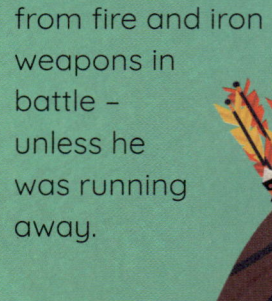

Payback from Permia
During his adventures, Odd made many enemies, including the people of Permia who he had stolen from when he was younger. To get their revenge, they created a terrible half-troll called Ogmund, who became Odd's arch-enemy. Ogmund was a dishonourable, treacherous menace and killed many of Odd's closest friends, his brother, Thord, and his half-giant son.

From the Depths

Whilst sailing through Greenland in pursuit of Ogmund, Odd and his crew stumbled upon two rocks floating in the ocean. Later that day, they were baffled when the rocks disappeared. They turned out to be the jaws of Sea-Mist, a great sea monster who swallowed whales and ships whole. Odd's seafaring encounters continued when a small band of his men went to explore a mysterious island covered in heather. When they landed ashore, the island rumbled violently and submerged, taking the crew with it. This living landmass was Heatherback, a giant creature summoned by Ogmund.

Tempting Fate

At the age of 300, Odd had defeated many enemies, man and monster alike, but he had grown homesick. Odd returned to his homeland, and walked over the grave of his old steed, Faxi, mocking the gods for the silly witch's curse that had troubled him all his life. It was at this moment that Odd tripped on Faxi's skull, disturbing a deadly viper that had nested inside. The serpent bit Odd, killing him, and the witch's tragic prophecy was fulfilled.

OVER THE SEA

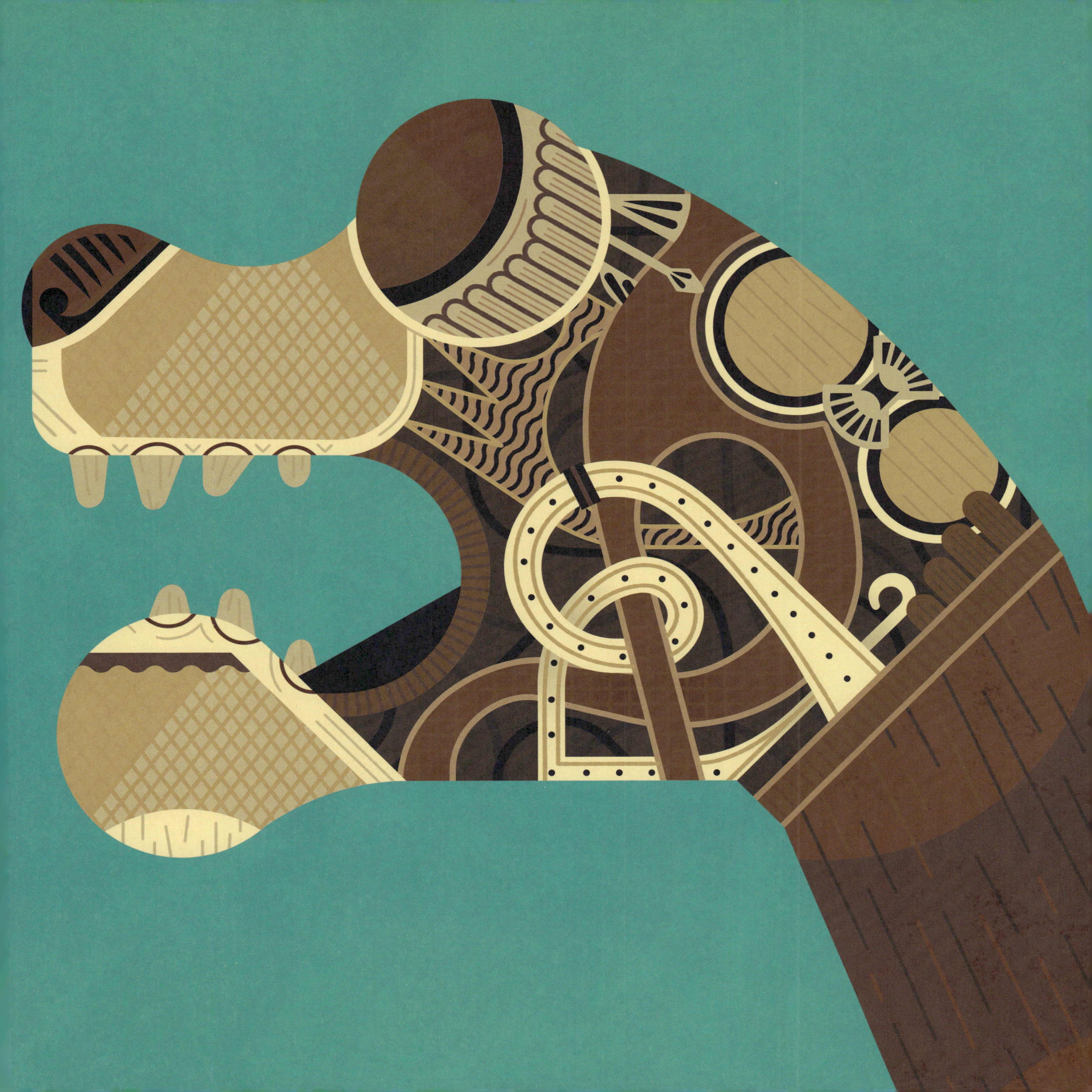

The Viking chief Erik the Red landed on Greenland in 982 after being exiled from Norway and Iceland. He named this land an appealing name – 'the green land' – to persuade more people to settle there. Fourteen ships carrying families, animals and building materials successfully made the journey from Iceland and they set up the first European settlement on the island. It remained until the 1400s.

It is thought that around the end of the 800s, more than 10,000 Vikings arrived and settled in Iceland. They were greeted by fertile farmland, wild forests and seas teeming with fish.

GOING PLACES

At the end of the 700s, Scandinavians began their expansion in waves. At first, small bands of Viking warriors set sail, sacking towns and cities on foreign shores, then returned to Scandinavia in the winter. Through the 800s, the numbers of Vikings going on expeditions grew into larger forces, who began to settle in the lands they once raided, setting up homes, farms, forts and trading hubs.

Britain felt the full force of Viking invaders, starting in 793 with the raid on the island of Lindisfarne. The raiders seized towns, including Dublin, Ireland, in 841. Dublin became a thriving Viking trading town with links to many other countries.

In 1001, a crew of Viking explorers led by Leif the Lucky, son of Erik the Red, were the first Europeans to set foot in North America, which they named Vinland. Soon after, a small group of Vikings went on to settle on the Canadian island now known as Newfoundland. However, they quickly abandoned their homes after clashes with local people.

In 859, a Viking expedition of 62 ships led by the king of Sweden, Björn Ironside, raided ancient cities in Spain, and towns around the Mediterranean coasts and Northern Africa.

Viking Sailing Routes

- 700s
- 800s
- 900s
- 1000s

Indigenous people of northern Scandinavia and surrounding areas called Sàmi traded with the Vikings. Today, the Sàmi still live a very similar life to their ancestors.

In the east, Vikings were called 'Rus', which is the origin of the word 'Russia'. Following the rivers in eastern Europe, the Rus' looted the lands surrounding their routes and the shores of the Caspian Sea from the 800s to 1000s.

What is now France and its neighbouring countries were victim to many Viking raids during the 800s. In 885, Viking forces relentlessly attacked Paris for an entire year, but they failed to capture the city.

A stone lion once stood in the Greek port of Piraeus, and a mischievous Viking vandal inscribed it with long looping bands of runes.

Scandinavians traded exotic goods in the deserts of the Middle East, but the riches of the close-by city of Constantinople (in the northwest of present-day Turkey) tempted other Vikings. Rus' forces ransacked the outskirts of Constantinople in 860, but retreated soon after. Some Viking warriors later returned to the city to become members of the Varangian Guard – highly trained bodyguards to wealthy emperors.

SCANDINAVIA · FINLAND · RUSSIA · EASTERN EUROPE · CASPIAN SEA · ITALY · MEDITERRANEAN SEA · GREECE · TURKEY · AFRICA · EGYPT · MIDDLE EAST

43

Life on Board
A Viking sailor's life out on the open sea was gruelling. When there was not enough wind to fill the ship's sail, the crew rowed with long wooden oars. Rough seas claimed many vessels, so crews didn't sail in the winter, instead waiting for the more favourable conditions of springtime to raid and trade by boat. Cats kept the crew company on board, catching rats and mice.

Seafaring Silver
Some Viking Age coins bear the image of boats, highlighting how important they were in Viking society.

Ferocious Fleets
A formidable warring Viking fleet that attacked France in 885 is said to have had around 300 ships.

Cut and Run
The Viking longship was a symbol of power and wealth. Its long shape allowed it to reach speeds of 28 kilometres per hour; its flat hull meant it could sail on shallow rivers as well as open seas; its lightness meant it could be carried over land; and its size meant it could hold 60 or more warriors. For added protection, sailors hung their shields over the edges as they rowed. Longships were used in 'lightning raids' – fast raids carried out before dawn on towns and monasteries to catch them by surprise. Once ashore, raiders plundered all the valuables they could carry, before hastily departing on their longships.

A carved dragon head from Oseberg, Norway

Curious Carvings
Longships usually featured a carved dragon or animal head at the bow and the stern. Vikings believed these decorative figureheads warded off evil spirits, but they would have also helped to instil fear into their enemies. The Oseberg ship burial, in Norway, contained five exquisite carved figureheads and the ship itself featured a coiled serpent's head at the bow and stern, as seen on the longship above.

VOYAGING VESSELS

The seafaring Scandinavians of the Viking Age owe much of their exploration success to the boats they sailed in. They skilfully designed and built many types of vessel, from small rowing boats called faerings, to the iconic longships that were used for war. The longship known as Skuldelev 2, which is one of five eleventh-century vessels found in Denmark, is longer than a blue whale! Propelled by wind or oars, boats allowed the Vikings to navigate rivers, fjords and the open oceans.

Blue Whale

Skuldelev 2

Precious Cargo
Shipbuilders constructed cargo ships called Knarrs, capable of transporting large loads, including goods for trade, supplies to reinforce battling Viking armies or building materials for new settlements overseas. Knarrs could hold up to 24 tonnes – the same weight as four African elephants.

Boat Building

Crafting a longship was no easy task. First, boat builders needed to find tall, sturdy trees to cut down. Like most Viking vessels, longships were 'clinker-built', which means their hull was constructed from overlapping planks fixed together with iron rivets. The sails were sometimes coated with animal fat to protect them, and plant fibres, animal hair or hides were twisted together to make the ropes. Finally, any holes were plugged with a mixture of fur or moss and sticky tar.

Logs were split into wedges for planks

Nautical Navigation

With no modern navigational tools, Viking mariners navigated using the Sun and stars. To head west from Scandinavia, towards England and the Atlantic Ocean, ships followed the sunset. To go east, ships aimed for the direction of the sunrise, which meant they were heading home. At night, sailors read the position of the stars to determine the direction they were heading in. Caged ravens were sometimes taken on board, too. If the raven flew in a direct path when it was released it was most likely heading for land, so the sailors eagerly followed.

The Uunartoq Disc

In 1948, a millennium-old wooden half-disc was discovered in Uunartoq, Greenland. Some historians believe it to be a primitive sun dial-like 'sun compass' used by early Scandinavians to help navigate the oceans. A pin in the centre of the disc would have cast a shadow, showing the direction (as shown right). Scientists think Vikings sailors may have also used crystals, which create light from a small amount of sunshine to help locate the Sun in cloudy conditions.

Sun disc (reconstructed)

Crystal

TREASURES FROM AFAR

Historians and archaeologists have unearthed many fascinating artefacts that show us just how widespread the Vikings' trading network was. From Mediterranean wine to exotic spices, traders travelled great distances to obtain goods from as far east as Central Asia. When they returned home, the traders sold their imports to wealthy Scandinavians for large sums.

The Slave Trade
Slaves or thralls were traded at a high price. Vikings took slaves from raids in foreign lands or at home, where certain crimes were punished with slavery.

Fair Trades
Early Scandinavians paid in chopped-up bullion (precious metals, mainly silver, but sometimes gold) and jewellery, and the trader weighed payments on a set of scales to ensure a fair deal was struck. Coins were adopted as currency in the 900s. The Vikings exported their local produce, such as home-grown foods, timber, animals and treasures from raids. They were masterful merchants and some famously tricked gullible customers by selling narwhal tusks as mythical unicorn horns for close to the price of gold!

The Wider World
Viking merchants bought goods including spices, glass and silk from the Middle East, wine and pottery from the Mediterranean and jewellery from India. There is no evidence that the Vikings travelled to China or India, but they established trade ties with many parts of Asia.

The Helgö Buddha
Perhaps one of the most extraordinary exotic objects discovered from the Viking Age is a small, bronze Buddha, found in Helgö, Denmark. This meditating figure dates back to the 500s. It was crafted in North India and brought into Scandinavia, travelling thousands of miles on board a ship to find its way into a wealthy Viking home. Among the same hoard was an ornate top piece of a religious staff from Ireland and a bronze ladle from North Africa.

Trading Towns
Bustling trading centres became established across Scandinavia, which had ties to far-flung places. The largest Scandinavian trade towns were Hedeby and Ribe in Denmark, Birka in Sweden and Kaupang in Norway. These were tempting targets for other Scandinavian raiders, so Viking chiefs offered protection to merchants for heavy taxes in return. The Rus' Vikings established their own thriving hubs along Russian rivers such as the Dnieper and Volga, with trade links to parts of Central Asia.

VIKING WARRIORS

Famously ferocious Viking warriors were feared by many. From the late 700s to around 1000, raiding expeditions happened often as the Vikings pushed to expand into new lands. This meant more and more warriors, who could be as young as 11 years old, were needed to fight. Raiding was considered an honourable occupation for young men seeking to prove themselves and return home with great riches. Viking warriors were not only tough in their physical strength but also in their mind – they believed that if they died bravely in battle they would go straight to the glorious Valhalla or Fólkvangr. When warriors weren't raiding, they were working as farmers, merchants, blacksmiths and craftsmen. When called upon, they followed their chief or king into battle.

Weapons of Choice
Vikings fought on foot in hand-to-hand combat. Most wielded a spear, wore lightweight leather armour and carried a round wooden shield painted with a Viking design. Wealthy warriors carried swords and were equipped with sturdy chain-mail armour, metal helmets and beautifully decorated weapons that displayed their success and status. Some Vikings even gave their weapons names, such as 'Leg-Biter' – a sword that features in the Icelandic *Laxdæla* saga, and 'Viper' – a sword that belonged to famous Viking poet and warrior, Egil Skallagrimsson.

Going Berserk
The most terrifying and brutal Viking warriors were known as berserkers. They had no fear of pain or death and some writings say they were gifted with unnatural powers by the god, Odin. Berserkers wore no armour, but instead dressed themselves in bear skins (the word berserker means 'bear coats'). Ancient accounts tell how berserkers performed a pre-battle ritual that sent them into a violent frenzy, making them bite the edge of their shields and howl at their enemies like wild animals.

Rebels with a Cause
So why did the Vikings decide to expand their territory from the late 700s? The freezing lands of Scandinavia meant that life was tough, especially in winter when farming was limited. Raids and expeditions provided opportunities for Scandinavians to settle in new places with milder climates and better farmland. A growing population may have also been a factor. Some raids, however, were simply to get rich! The money and treasures collected were too tempting and provided a fast track to fame and fortune.

MEDIEVAL WARFARE

The brutal raid on a holy coastal island in northeast England called Lindisfarne in 793 was the event that marked the beginning of the Viking Age. Larger raids followed shortly after and soon word spread of the terror of these attacks. Europe's struggle against Viking invaders began.

The Viking Great Army
Less than a century after the first raid, Viking tribes across Sweden, Norway and Denmark that once fought against each other joined up to form a formidable force, known as the Viking Great Army. Historians debate the exact number, but it is thought to have been made up of 3,000 battle-ready warriors. In 865, the Viking Great Army invaded England and captured the city of Eoforwic, now York, in 866. Over the next 30 years, the army split into two, with one force moving north and one south. In Britain they battled against the Anglo-Saxons. In the late 800s, many kingdoms across Europe fortified their defences to protect themselves against Viking forces.

Paying for Peace
Rather than putting up a fight, some rulers bribed the Vikings into leaving their kingdoms alone. In 886, a Frankish king called Charles the Fat paid raiders to leave Paris and devastate nearby areas instead. However, it wasn't long before the Vikings returned to Paris and attempted another attack.

Cnut the Great

Sweyn Forkbeard and his youngest son, Cnut, invaded England in 1013. Sweyn succeeded where so many Vikings before him had failed and took the English throne that Christmas, uniting Denmark, Norway and England. However, the new king died just five weeks later, which triggered a dispute for the throne between Cnut and other Anglo-Saxon rulers. After three years of campaigning, Cnut was victorious and became king of England in 1016.

A Royal Family

Cnut's great grandfather was Gorm the Old, king of Denmark from 936 to 958. Gorm's son, Harald Bluetooth, succeeded him to the throne in 958 and united all of Denmark under a Christian rule. In 986, Sweyn Forkbeard, son of Harald and father of Cnut, seized the Danish throne.

The Old Gods

King Cnut did not worship the Norse gods as his ancestors had – instead, he chose to become a Christian. Christianity had spread in northern Europe and many parts of Scandinavia were united under a Christian rule, so many Vikings were abandoning their traditional Norse beliefs.

THE END OF AN AGE

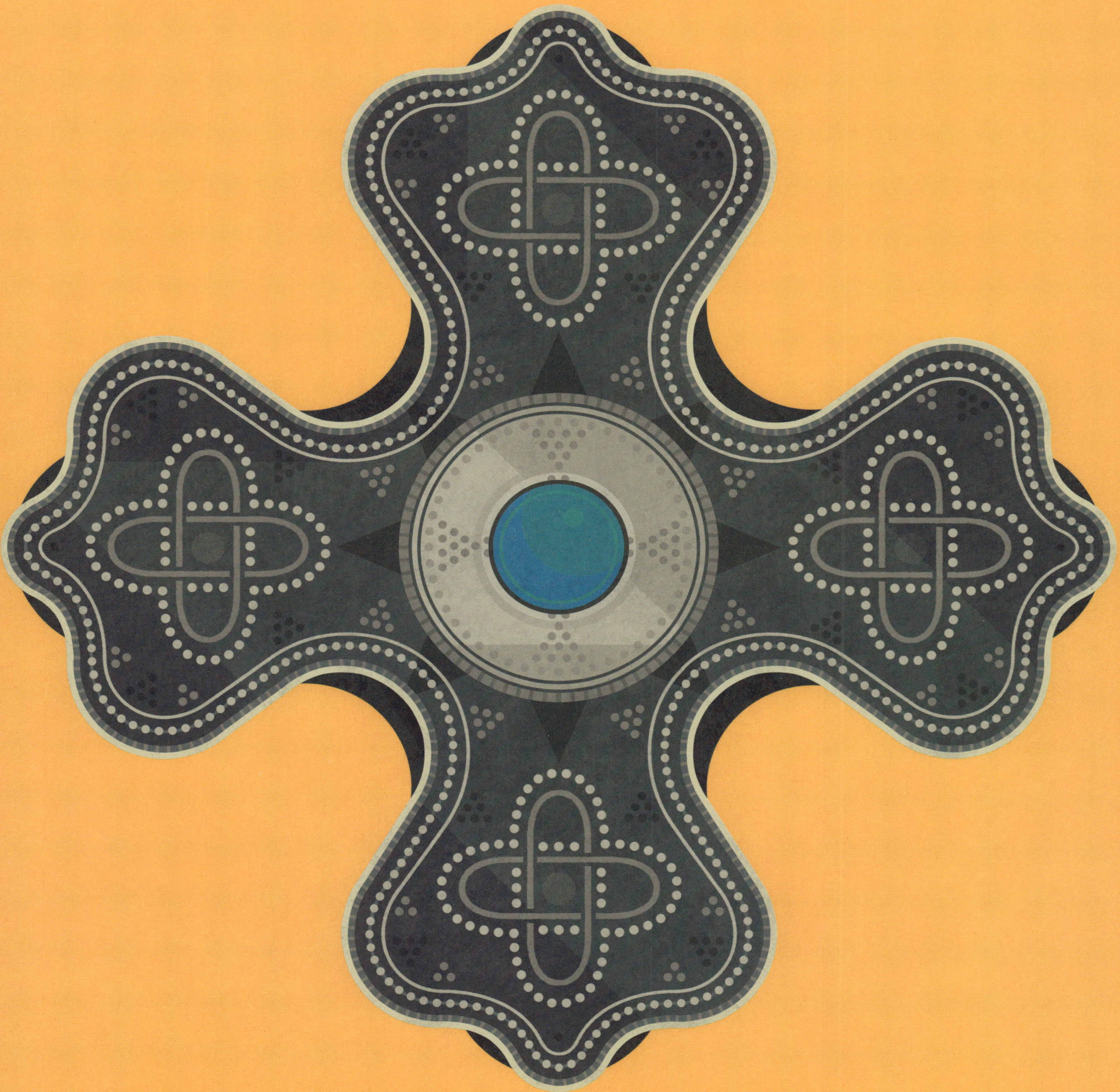

BREAKING FAITH

From as early as the 800s, the Christian faith had slowly begun to gnaw at the roots of the Norse way of life. It spread, becoming the dominant faith in Scandinavia by the 1000s, marking the beginning of the end of the Viking Age. As well as a change of religion, historians say that several other factors sealed the Vikings' fate.

Putting Down Roots
Vikings who settled in lands where Christianity was the religion converted so they could farm and start families peacefully. They swapped their colourful Norse gods for the one Christian God and abandoned old Norse religious ceremonies, including sacrifices and boat burial funerals, that were once a vital part of their lives.

Striking Deals
Some Viking leaders embraced Christianity for political gains. A relentless Viking raider named Rollo converted to Christianity in 911. In return, the Frankish king, Charles the Simple, gifted him the French region of Normandy to rule over and defend from other Viking raiders.

Christian Conversions

Christian missionaries from across Europe travelled through Scandinavia, converting Vikings to their faith. Old Norse temples and statues were torn down by newly Christian kings, and replaced with ornate Viking-styled wooden stave churches. More than 1,000 stave churches were built across Scandinavia, but less than 30 remain today.

The Faith of a Nation

King Harald Bluetooth declared Denmark a Christian nation around 965, after he agreed to be baptised. It is unclear if he truly believed in the faith or if this was simply a political move, because Denmark's powerful Christian neighbour, the Holy Roman Empire, threatened to convert Denmark and all its people by force. Both Norway and Sweden followed suit soon after, adopting Christianity in the 1100s.

A FINAL BLOW

The Viking Age ended in 1066 when the Norwegian king Harald Hardrada and his forces were crushed as they attempted to claim the English throne from King Harold Godwinson. Only 19 days later and still fresh from victory, King Harold and his forces were defeated by the invading Duke of Normandy, William the Conqueror, in the Battle of Hastings. Some of these events are told on the Bayeux Tapestry, a famous embroidery made in England. It measures an impressive 70 metres long and was created around 1070 for the Norman king.

The Last Raids
Many historians declare the end of the Viking Age with Harald Hardrada in 1066, but scattered raids continued for another hundred years or so, ending in the 1100s. The Vikings weren't conquered – they simply lived in Christian societies at home or in new settlements set up by the Vikings. The ruthless raiding that Scandinavians once terrorised Europe with was no longer profitable, and European kings organised their defences and armies to handle raiders, so the Vikings took up a more civil life.

Prose Edda
An Icelandic poet and historian by the name of Snorri Sturluson (1179–1241), collected ancient Viking stories throughout his lifetime, offering us a greater insight into their culture and mythology. Snorri compiled many of his texts into books long after the Viking Age had ended. One such book thought to have been written by Snorri is the *Prose Edda*, which describes the fascinating Norse gods and their legendary stories, from the creation of the cosmos to Ragnarök.

The Battle of Hastings

There was no time for the English king Harold to celebrate the victory because William the Conqueror and his army had firmly planted themselves in southern England. The exhausted English forces immediately marched south, and battled with the invaders on 14 October 1066, near Hastings. King Harold was killed and his army devastated, with soldiers attempting to flee amidst the violence. By December, the Normans had taken all of England, and on Christmas Day William was crowned king. William was the great-great-great-grandson of Rollo, the Viking raider turned Christian ruler who had been gifted the region of Normandy by Charles the Simple.

The Battle of Stamford Bridge

Harald Hardrada had fought all across eastern Europe and the Mediterranean as part of the Varangian Guard, before becoming the sole King of Norway in 1047. To take England from King Harold Godwinson, he assembled a 9,000-strong army of warriors and formed an alliance with Tostig Godwinson, the English king's own brother. At the village of Stamford Bridge, in Yorkshire, England, the armies clashed and thousands of warriors were killed, including both Harald Hardrada and Tostig. This loss was the last Viking invasion into Europe – the Viking Age was over.

THE VIKINGS' LEGACY

Ending around 1,000 years ago, the influence of the Viking Age can still be felt far and wide, from European languages to trade routes still used today. The Vikings adapted to the Christian world and live on to this day, several generations later.

Wandering Souls
The Vikings settled in many lands, establishing significant places along the way, such as Iceland, which still has a deeply rooted Viking heritage. In the 900s, Viking invaders founded Dublin, the modern capital of Ireland, transforming it into a bustling trading city that they ruled over until the 1100s.

The Gods' Gift
One of the most enduring gifts left behind by the Vikings is their tales of outlandish gods, crafty dwarves, shape-shifting giants, nasty trolls and greedy dragons. This has captured the imaginations of adults and children alike, influencing many of J. R. R. Tolkien's iconic books, including *The Hobbit*, Marvel's *Thor* series and countless other books, movies, TV shows and video games.

War of Words

Invading Scandinavians also brought their language to the shores of many European countries, and Old Norse words still form a part of their languages, including English. 'Law', 'leg' and even 'glitter' – coming from 'glit', meaning shining, or bright – stem from Old Norse. Some days of the week are named after Norse gods – Thursday comes from 'Thor's day', Tuesday from 'Tyr's day' and Friday from 'Frigg's day'.

An Unfinished Story

There is a lot that isn't fully understood about the Vikings. How much of North America did they explore? Why did they abandon Greenland in the 1400s? Archaeologists and historians are still piecing together their story as they discover new artefacts all over the globe. There is still a lot to learn about the Viking voyagers.

GLOSSARY

Æsir – A groups of Norse gods that includes Odin and Thor.

Adorn – To add something decorative or impressive.

Agriculture – The practice of farming.

Ancient – Dating back to the distant past.

Ancestor – A relative that lived a long time ago.

Anglo-Saxon – The people of England during medieval times.

Antler – The branching structure that usually grows on the heads of animals such as deer.

Archaeologist – The study and science of human history.

Artefact – Some type of object made by a human, usually of historical importance.

Brooch – A piece of jewellery that fastens clothes together.

Cargo – Trading goods carried on some form of transportation such as a boat.

Carpenter – The trade of making or fixing wooden structures, furniture and objects.

Ceremony – A celebrated or public ritual or event with great importance.

Christian – A person who believes in the teachings of Jesus Christ.

Clan – A close-knit group of people with a common goal or close relation.

Colony – An area or group of people settling under one rule or nationality.

Culture – The behaviour, beliefs, way of life and customs of a civilization or people of a particular time.

Currency – The system of exchange used in a particular place, such as money.

Dialect – Language in a specific place, time, religion or group of people.

Deity – A god or goddess, such as Thor, Odin and Idunn.

Domesticate – Taming an animal for use on a farm or as a pet e.g. dog

Draugr – An undead person or spirit originating from Norse mythology.

Dwarf – A mysterious being from Norse mythology who was skilled at smithing (metal working).

Expedition – A journey undertaken by a group of people, usually with a specific goal e.g. exploration, war.

Faith – Strong belief in a religion.

Figurine – A small, human-like model.

Fjord – A deep body of water between mountains and cliffs, and many are found in Norway, Denmark and Sweden.

Folklore – Traditional myths, tales and beliefs relating to a group of people.

Francia – Also known as the Frankish Empire, the area that covered what is modern-day France.

Hearth – A brick, stone or wooden fireplace, also used as the cooking area in Viking homes.

Hilt – The handle of any weapon or tool, such as a sword or hammer.

Hoard – A large collection or store of valuable objects.

Holy – Something considered very special due to religious importance.

Inscribe – To carve or write letters, words or symbols on an object.

Ivory – The substance that the tusks of animals, such as elephants or walruses, are made of.

Jarl – A noble Viking chief or ruler.

Karl – Middle-class people in early Scandinavian society, usually farmers or landowners.

Kingdom – A place under a King or Queen's rule.

Livestock – Animals kept on a farm for food, milk or other purposes.

Longship – A narrow, long warship sailed by the Vikings.

Loom – A tool for weaving fabric.

Loot – Stealing goods and property.

Mead – A honey-based alcoholic drink.

Medieval – Related to the Middle Ages, a European period of history spanning from roughly 600 to 1500.

Mercenary – A soldier hired to serve a foreign cause or in an army.

Merchandise – Objects and goods that are brought and sold in business.

Mineral – A substance that occurs naturally, such as rock or crystal.

Missionary – Somebody on a quest to promote their religion in other places.

Monastery – A place in which devout religious people live and worship.

Mythology – A set of stories belonging to a particular religion or culture.

Naval – Related to boats and warships.

Norse – Relating to Scandinavia in ancient times.

Ornament – A decorative item with no practical purpose other than to look decorative.

Pagan – Belonging to a religion with many gods.

Plank – A long, flat piece of wood.

Prophecy – A prediction for the future.

Raid – A surprise assault on an enemy.

Relic – An ancient object of extreme cultural or historic interest.

Rune – Any symbol or letter from the alphabet from ancient Europe and Scandinavia.

Sacrifice – The act of killing an animal or person as a religious offering.

Saga – Long stories from ancient Scandinavian societies, usually telling of heroic adventures.

Scandinavia – The region of northern Europe that includes the countries of Sweden, Norway and Denmark.

Settler – Someone who travels to a new land to start a new life.

Talisman – An object believed to have supernatural or magical powers.

Temple – A building for worshipping a god or gods.

Thatch – A material, usually used for roofing and made of straw, leaves, reeds and similar foliage.

Thrall – In medieval Scandinavia, a slave, servant or captive.

Trinket – An ornament or piece of jewellery usually small in size.

Troll – Originating from Old Norse, an ugly monster-like creature that usually lives in a cave.

Tunic – Loose clothing that reaches the knees and covers the body.

Vanir – A tribe of gods featured in Norse mythology and associated with magic, fertility and wisdom.

Vessel – Some type of ship, boat or other water craft.

Worship – The act of honouring a god, sometimes in a ceremony.